F McPherson

Geological Sketch of the Province of Cadiz

F McPherson

Geological Sketch of the Province of Cadiz

ISBN/EAN: 9783337096878

Printed in Europe, USA, Canada, Australia, Japan

Cover: Foto ©ninafisch / pixelio.de

More available books at **www.hansebooks.com**

GEOLOGICAL SKETCH

OF THE

PROVINCE OF CADIZ

BY

J. Mc Pherson.

ABSTRACT OF A SIMILAR WORK WRITTEN BY THE AUTHOR
IN SPANISH.

———————•◆•———————

CADIZ.
—
PRINTED BY FEDERICO JOLY,
REVISTA MEDICA.
1873.

LIMITS AND CLIMATE

OF THE PROVINCE.

The Province of Cadiz occupies the southern extremity of the Iberian Peninsula. It extends from 36° to 37° N. Lat. and from 1° 25 to 2° 45 W. Long. of the Madrid Meridian. Its total surface amounts to 7.275 square kilometers.

From the mouth of the Guadalquivir to the straits of Gibraltar its coasts form a series of parallel lines receding towards the east and constantly alineated from N.N.W. to S.S.E. whilst from Tarifa to the Bay of Gibraltar they take exactly an opposite direction.

This constant direction of the western coast is, as it will be seen in the sequel, intimately connected with one of the most important geological phenomena to be observed in this region.

The climate of this Province is considerably cooler than that which it might be inferred would correspond to its latitude.

The mean temperature of the coast is scarcely higher than 17°5 centigrade, consequently the isothermal line of 20 centigrade, which touches in the Algarbes and in the Province of Malaga, describes a great curve the concavity of which follows the direction of the coast.

The annexed tables show the result of the Meteorological observations taken at the Observatory of San Fernando and at Tarifa from the year 1866 to 1870.

	BAROMETER.			TEMPERATURE CENTIGR.							RAIN	
	Mean.	Max.	Min.	Mean year.	Mean winter.	Mean spring.	Mean summ.	Mean aut.	Max.	Min.	Amount in Mill.	Days.
SAN FERNANDO. 28m												
1866-67	761.3	774.1	742.3	18.5	14.1	17.2	23.3	19.5	37.	1.2	901.5	85
1867-68	761.9	773.4	745.6	17.2	11.9	16.8	22.6	17.6	36.2	-0.6	999.1	98
1868-69	762.2	774.8	746.5	17.7	12.9	15.5	23.6	18.7	38.1	3.6	480.9	87
1869-70	760.5	772.8	738.4	18.3	12.9	16.9	23.9	19.5	35.7	0.2	956.9	96
	761.4	773.7	743.2	17.9	12.9	16.6	23.3	18.8	36.7	1.1	834.6	91
TARIFA. 15m												
1866-67	761.8	773.5	745.7	18.1	13.4	17.3	23.	18.8	34.	0.9	494.7	54
1867-68	762.4	773.3	748.5	17.	12.3	16.2	23.1	16.5	32.6	-0.4	771.9	71
1868-69	762.5	774.8	747.2	17.2	12.9	15.3	22.4	18.4	32.2	3.0	443.9	60
1869-70	761.2	773.6	740.8	16.7	11.6	15.5	21.4	18.3	31.9	3.0	600.2	87
	761.9	773.8	745.5	17.2	12.5	16.1	22.4	18.	32.7	1.6	578.5	68

The year is divided into two seasons, the dry and the rainy: the first commences in the beginning of June and lasts till the middle of September. The distribution of rain, even during the rainy season, is extremely unequal. Sometimes more than the third of the total fall of the year is poured in torrents during seven or eight days and on other occasions whole months pass without a drop of rain.

For instance from 31 October to 7 November 1871 the rain gauge at San Fernando measured 334 milimeters of rain or more than the third of the total fall of the year.

The winds in this region generally blow strongly and are at times extremely inconvenient. The south and S.W. winds are always damp in winter and are accompanied with rains and gales which though rarely are felt with great violence specially in the vicinity of the straits. These gales naturally depend on the course which the storms follow on their way from the Ocean to the coasts of Europe. Those which are felt with the greatest intensity are dependant on the storms whose centres pass by the north of Spain, but even those which reach Europe [by the north of Ireland are occasionally felt with great violence in this locality.

The truly disagreeable wind is the east or levante which sometimes during summer blows hardly without intermission.

In this period of the year it sometimes blows for ten or fifteen consecutive days. It is intensely hot and dry and at times blows with such extreme force as to uproot trees.

This wind generally subsides at daybreak and gradually increases as the day advances. Its dry and burning qualities have been referred to the wind blown sands of Africa, but on studying its conditions it will be clearly seen that they are dependant on the special situation of this part of the continent.

This wind blows during three different states of the atmosphere. In two of them nearly always during winter in the other during the summer months, and this can be considered as the normal wind. In the first case the levante blows when revolving storms pass to the south of the straits.

In the second when storms exist to the westward of the Spanish coasts, when even in winter it blows with great force, and thirdly when none of these circumstances occur, which is the most frequent case with the levantes in summer. When a levante blows in summer, as a rule the atmospheric state of the countries surrounding the straits is the following. In the Mediterranean and in the coast of Algeria the wind blows from the N. E. whilst in the Mediterranean coasts of Spain it blows from the S. E. and in the vicinity of the straits due east with extreme violence. It is here felt as an extremely cool and damp wind and a band of clouds is formed in all the surrounding mountains.

On the other side of the mountains the characters of this wind completely change; it becomes extremely dry and hot and its velocity gradually deminishes till in the limits of the Province of Seville it is rarely felt.

Situated at the Pico del Algibe whilst a strong levante was blowing I have been able to observe this change perfectly well.

From this isolated peak the blue Mediterranean could be seen, whilst thick cumulus were formed in the first spurs of the Sierra and driven by the wind envolved the Pico del Algibe in a thick mist which deposited an abundant dew on all this part of the Sierra. On crossing the watershed the mist was seen gradually to dissappear; at a short distance from the peak the sky was perfectly pure and from hence the wind commenced to acquire its hot and dry properties. Whilst these gales blow in the vicinity of the straits, the Castilles, the Mancha and the valley of the Guadalquivir are under the influence of calms or local winds.

On the coast of Portugal on the contrary, strong North and N. W, breezes predominate. The same phenomenon is observed in the coasts of Morocco, whilst at a short distance in the Atlantic the trade winds blow without interruption.

The most plausible explanation which occurs to me on observing this state of the atmosphere is the following. If no continent existed in this part of the world, the N. E. trade winds would blow during the summer months almost without intermission; but instead of this there exists not only Spain with its arid table lands but the African continent with its great Desert of Sahara.

These two parts of the earth under the influence of a nearly vertical sun are naturally intensely heated and both become, one with its desolate plains and the other with its barren sands, two inmense flues towards which the air rushes from all the surrounding regions, consequently the N. E. wind which blows in the Mediterranean finds itself solicited by these two columns of ascending air.

If it were only the central Spanish plateau what solicited the N. E. trade wind, this wind would blow in the vicinity of the straits as a S. E. wind, but as at the same time it is attracted by the burning African sands to the south, it has not only to take a resultant direction but it must also acquire a corresponding velocity to satisfy this double current of ascending air.

This attraction of the surrounding air, specially the one produced by the African continent does not completely disappear even during the winter months, therefore the whole of the levantes though produced by different causes obey more or less to its action.

The second case is likewise the result of this attraction, for the wind which would blow from the south or S. E. in conformity to the revolving motion of the storm if the African continent did not exist must be deflected to the south and blow as an east wind and acquire corresponding velocity to the magnitude of the two demands.

OROGRAPHICAL DESCRIPTION.

In the Spanish text of this work I precede the orographical description of the Province with a description of the orographical structure of the whole Peninsula, but in this abstract, which is principally for the information of foreigners, I do not consider it necessary to enter so fully into the details of the general structure of the country, and a brief summary of the most important orographical facts will be sufficient.

The Peninsula may be considered as a huge protuberance of a trapezoïdal form elevated upwards of 500 metres above the sea.

This protuberance is traversed by five great depressions which are the beds of as many rivers. These rivers are separated from each other by a series of mountains which may be reduced to six great groups, five of which run approximately from east to west. These are the Pyrenean and Cantabrian Chain, the Carpeto Vetonic Chain, the Oretanian Chain and the Marianic and Betic Chains, which run parallel to each other from the shores of the Mediterranean to those of the Atlantic. The last of these chains terminates its southern slopes directly in the Mediterranean opposite the African coast.

The sixth group or Celtiberian Chain extends in a SE. direction from the Cantabrian Chain in the Province of Santander to the shores of the Mediterranean in the Kingdom of Valencia, cutting all the other chains almost at right angles.

The Geological study of this Province only embraces the southwest extreme of the Betican Chain.

This Chain runs parallel to the Sierra Morena or Marianic Chain and between them flows the River Guadalquivir.

The structure of the Sierra Morena Mountains is very remarkable. The succession of hills which constitute it have their origin in the great tertiary plains of the Province of Albacete.

Its beginning can be traced as already shewn by M. M. Verneuil and Collomb to the depression through which, between Villanueva de la Reina and Vianos, the river Guadarmena flows, and the protuberance of Silurian deposits in the centre of the valley constitutes the commencement of the Marianic Chain.

In its beginning the watershed between the rivers Guadiana and Guadalquivir follows a nearly level tract of ground, but from near Despeñaperros the country becomes extremely wild and grand, specially in the savage gorges of this celebrated pass.

After this change in the orographical structure of the country the waters flow in a very extraordinary manner.

The watershed of the rivers Guadiana and Guadalquivir, instead of following those series of hills, keeps at their back on the borders of the great plains of La Mancha, whilst the waters which flow from the Northern slopes of these hills, after following sometime the valleys which these ridges form between each other, strike to the south and flow into the Guadalquivir.

What is seen at Despeñaperros, where the distortion of the strata are very extraordinary, as it may be seen by referring to section N.º 1, is constantly repeated in the whole length of this chain. The descent to the valley of the Guadalquivir from the watershed in the plains of La Mancha and Estremadura is constantly through a series of abrupt and wild gorges. This abnormal structure, united to the state of great distortion in which the strata are found, as well as the difference of level which exist between the marine tertiary deposits of Estremadura and the valley of the Guadalquivir, and the numerous patches of this formation which at different levels are found through the innermost recesses of the Sierra Morena according to M. E. Thierry, make it highly probable that the structure of this chain is due to a series of faults, which coinciding perhaps with the upheaval of the central plateau of the Peninsula, have given to this country its present extraordinary structure. Unhappily facts are too scant to allow of the complete elucidation of this interesting subject, but when describing the disturbances which this Province has experienced I will further revert to it.

The Betic Chain has its origin in the great protuberance formed by Capes La Nao and San Antonio and extends in a broad belt to the coast of the Ocean in the Province of Cadiz.

This group of mountains ought with reference to its orographical structure to be considered as only one, but geologically, as some geologists have already done, they constitute two distinct systems.

The series of mountains which stretch from Cape La Nao to the Province of Cadiz are known as the Betic Chain, and the series of litoral heights more or less parallel to the coast, which extend from the Province of Almeria to that of Malaga, as the Penibetic Chain.

The characteristic feature of the Betic system specially, is that it does not constitute a true chain or Cordillera, but is formed by a series of parallel ridges which are not only separated and cut through by the rivers which descend from the Penibetic Chain to the south, but by the waters which flow from their southern slopes and which after running some time between these parallel ridges, cut through them nearly at right angles and flow into the Guadalquivir.

These parallel links are connected to each other by a series of arid and elevated wastes, which separate the waters of the Guadalquivir from those which flow into the Mediterranean.

The mean direction of the Betican Chain is E. 28°N. parallel to the broad belt of Secondary and Numulitic deposits which with a mean breadth of 60 kilometers occupies all the south of the Peninsula.

The Penibetic system, which comprises the highest summits of the Peninsula in the Sierra Nevada, follows more or less an east to west direction and is formed almost exclusively of mica-schists and dolomites. It follows the coast from the Province of Almeria to the Serrania de Ronda, where both systems are blended together in the great and intricate mass of mountains known under that name.

The description of a part of these mountains is the special object of this paper. This huddle of mountains constitute the mass of Sierras between the right bank of the Guadalhorce and the coasts of the ocean. This part of the system is divided by the river Guadiaro into two distinct groups, the left side group forming the culminating point of the whole Serrania, whilst those on the right side constitute the mountains of this Province.

The structure of the mountains which constitute the group of this Province is the result of a series of geological disturbances which, as it will be seen in the sequel, have all more or less contributed to give it its present wild and disconnected appearance.

Prior to the Tertiary epoch the Secondary deposits appear to have been sufficiently upheaved to form a protuberance or an archipelago of sufficient dimensions to efficiently influence the deposits of the Tertiary sea. All the sediments to the North of this protuberance are extremely soft and incoherent, whilst those deposited to the south are extremely hard and compact. During the Pliocene period or perhaps even during part of the Miocene epoch the entire strata was contorted in a series of parallel folds.

Coincident with this disturbance and on the anticlinal axis of these folds numerous eruptions of greenstone took place, and the strata in the vicinity of these rocks was exposed to a mineralizing action which completely altered them into gypsums, dolomites and variegated clays. These comparatively soft strata were easily destroyed by atmospheric agencies, and therefore the erosions as a rule have followed the anticlinal axis of the folds, which consequently form the greatest depressions of the country.

Previous to these crests having been degraded to their present level, the troughs of the folds which at that period formed the valleys of the country were covered by a red diluvial deposit which still accupies a great extent of Andalusia.

Inmediatcly after this diluvial deposit had taken place this region experienced another very violent disturbance.

Exactly at right angles to the direction of the folds, which is E. 28 N. this region appears to have been wrenched asunder, and all its strata was fissured in a series of fractures which are parallel to the coast, and which subsequently have been considerably enlarged through erosions of vast magnitude.

When the above resumé of circunstances is taken into account, it will be easily understood how extremely appropriate they must be to produce a system of mountains as disconnected as those which constitute the group which raises beween the rivers Guadalete and Guadiaro. The essential character of these mountains, and specially of those formed by the Tertiary deposits, is that they neither form a definite range nor a series of detatched ridges parallel to the direction of the folds, as happens with the Jura Mountains, where the crest of the folds form as a rule the summits of the hills, and the troughs on the contrary the greatest depressions.

In this Province the foldings of the strata have been at times so near each other that frequently neither crest nor trough can be seen, whilst at other times, when the folds have been sufficiently ample to allow both crest and trough to be recognized, the crest has been degraded to the lowest level of the country, whilst the trough forms a hardly appreciable depression on the summits of the hills.

The difficulty of understanding this complicated structure, is still greatly enhanced through the fractures which at right angles appear to have broken asunder this series of already disconnected ridges.

These fractures, have caused a succession of extremely deep and broad parallel valleys, which separate some extremely rugged groups of mountains.

The summits of the totality of these mountains, are alineated from N. N. W. to S. S. E., parallel to the direction of the valleys, whilst the folding of the strata are perpendicular to them, and it is frequently observed when situated in these great transversal valleys, that the folds of one mountain correspond to those of the mountains on the other side of the valley. Even these already disconnected ridges do not form a continued crest, but are frequently separated by the deep depressions formed by the anticlinal axis.

These parallel segments, are united together either by disconnected hills, or by slightly rising plains, which form the watershed of the different rivers which flow from these mountains.

These rising plains or succession of low hills follow as a rule the direction E. 28 N. which the folds of the strata follow, and whilst the summits of these parallel segments reach 1000 or 900 meters, the connecting watersheds are hardly more than 100 to 150 meters above the sea.

The mass of mountains to the North of the river Guadiaro form two very distinct systems.

(2)

One of them is constituted by the series of isolated protuberances, in more or less undulating plains, which from the North
of the Meseta de Arriate and forming the watershed between the
Rivers Guadalete and Guadalquivir, extend to the coast of the
Atlantic between the mouths of these two rivers.

These protuberances are known under the names of Sierras
Terril, Montellano and Gibalbin, which latter Sierra terminates
in the low grounds to the North of Jerez.

The other group of mountains is comprehended between the
left bank of the Guadalete and the right of the Guadiaro. If the
annexed isometrical chart be referred to, it will be found that all
these mountains form four nearly isolated groups, separated by
deep intervening valleys which run from N. N. W. to S. S. E.

These groups are the following; the elevated summits to the
N. E. of the Province; the central mass of the Sierra del Algibe;
and the cluster of mountains known under the name of Sierras
del Campo de Gibraltar, which are divided into two groups by
the great depression of the Janda Lake. '

The first of these groups, is principally constituted by a great
protuberance of Secondary limestone 20 kilometers in lenght from
N. W. to S. E. and about seven kilometers in its mean breath,

The crest of these rocks are known under the name of Sierra
de Libar, Sierra del Endrinal, and Sierra del Pinar; this last Sierra
is the highest of the Province and reaches 1740 meters in the
Cerro del Pinar. The whole of this mass of Secondary rock consti-
titutes a nearly continuous crest of about 1.300 meters above the
sea, and from 400 to 500 meters above the Tertiary table lands
on the Ronda side.

From this mass some very important offshoots depart, one strikes
from the vicinity of Grazalema and with an E. N. E. direction is
incorporated to the high table land of Arriate.

Between this Tertiary ridge, which separates the waters of the
Guadiaro from those of the Guadalete, a remarkable occurrence
takes place.

The waters which collect in the valley formed by it and the
Sierra de Libar not finding a direct outlet to the valley of the Guadiaro, after penetrating through a wild and savage gorge disappear

under the mountain, till they again flow 3 miles to the S. W. on the other side of the Sierra at the Cueva del Gato near Benaojan.

Another very considerable ramification stretches from the N. W. extremity of the Sierra del Pinar in a W. S. W. direction to the. south of Arcos.

This part of the watershed of the Rivers Guadalete and Majaceite is constituted by a succession of hills of between 300 and 400 meters above the sea, which gradually deminish in height till they are lost in the plains of La Pedrosa to the south of Arcos where both rivers meet.

The most important sources of both these rivers, which considering their small basins possess a very considerable volume of water, are derived from the abundant springs which flow from both sides of this dislocated and broken mass of Secondary limestone.

From the southern extremity of this protuberance spring two more offshoots.

One of them striking to the South from the Sierra de Libar terminates near the town of Jimena, whilst the other unites the western extremity of this Sierra to the central group of mountains of the Province, where the Sierra del Algibe raises to upwards of of 1.100 meters.

These mountains form a kind of knot in the centre of the Province, from which numerous ridges strike in every direction, as it may be seen by referring to the isometrical chart.

To the south of the Sierra del Algibe these ridges soon blend into two parallel ones, which stretch towards the southeast and terminate near the Bay of Gibraltar. From the North of the Sierra, another one strikes to the N. W. and terminates near Tempul under the name of Sierra de las Cabras. The isolation and structure of this mountain, which is very remarkable may be seen in section N.º 18.

From the west of this Sierra, a series of hills and intervening plains stretch towards Cape Trafalgar, whilst from the south of the Pico del Algibe, a hilly tract of ground unites these mountains to the group of Sierras del Campo de Gibraltar.

These mountains form a series of parallel ridges which with the break of the Janda Lake stretch to the very shores of the

Atlantic. They form a series of most remarkable isolated mountains, formed of the upper Nummulitic sandstone and where the structure I have already described, of valleys at right angles to the folds of the strata can be observed to the greatest advantage.

DESCRIPTION OF THE SECONDARY ROCKS

The secondary deposits occupy in this region an extremely important position, as they constitute the summits of the principal mountains of the Province.

The most ancient strata of this locality, belong to the Liassic formation, though it is very probable that many of the gypsiferous rocks found at the base of the Jurassic formation may belong to the Triassic. But as it will be seen in the sequel many great anomalies would have to be explained if the whole of these deposits were to be considered Triassic, and therefore as no fossils have been found even in those which appear to protrude from under the Jurassic strata, I refrain from taking any notice of this formation.

The total of the secondary deposits of these regions form three distinct series of rocks perfectly well defined by their respective faunas. The one at the base is formed by strata which belong to the Liassic formation. In the second, organic remains are found which prove it to belong to the upper Jurassic series, whilst in the third, beginning with the fauna of Stramberg the strata terminate with true Neocomian deposits.

The Lias is constituted by two groups of rocks perfectly different.

The first is formed, by a great thickness of calcareous shales, which in a broad belt stretch from the village of Benamahoma to the Puerto del Pinar, and forming the base of the Cerro del Pinar on its Northwest side, disappear under the compact limestone ridge, which from near Grazalema runs in the direction of Zahara.

These shales vary in their color from a light gray to nearly black and are always extremely fissile.

Sometimes they are very bituminous and very frequently

small particles of mica are seen between the planes of clivage. In the lower part of these shales organic remains are rarely seen, with the exception of some badly preserved impressions of plants, but towards the upper part of the strata and where these shales become more compact, in passing to the limestones of the upper group in the Puerto del Pinar, it is frequent to find Ammonites in a fair state of preservation. Amongst them M. de Verneuil has determined the A. Bifrons, A. Complanata and A. Insignis. Besides these I have seen the A. Radians and others not yet determined.

Superposed to these shales, there comes another great thickness of compact limestone of a darkish gray colour, which in the summit of the Cerro del Pinar attain the considerable height of 1.700 meters.

It is difficult to find any organic remains in these limestones, and when they are found they are casts not easy to recognize; nevertheless it has been possible to determine the Spirifer Rostratus and at the Rock of Gibraltar, which is formed of this very limestone, the Eulyma Hedintonensis and the Terebratula Tetraedra have been found, fossils belonging to the upper Lias.

The total thickness of these limestones, judging from the differences of level at which they are seen, cannot be reckoned much under 500 meters.

These rocks, especially in the anticlinal axis of the valley of Benamahoma, are in some places reduced to minute fragments and cemented by carbonate of lime.

Through the influence of the atmosphere the cement decays more easily than the primitive rock, and the entire mass thus acquires an extraordinary brechiform appearance.

These limestones occupy a very considerable extension of land, and it may be asserted that they constitute the base of the whole Serrania in the N. E. of the Province.

She second great group is equally subdivided into two sub-groups, but unfortunately its lower strata are not so well determined as those of the first group.

Where these rocks attain their greatest development and where they naturally can be best studied is in the Sierra del Endrinal.

This group is composed at its base, of a considerable thickness of brick red and white marly shales.

All along the Manga de Villaluenga and from hence to Grazalema, similarly to what happens in the Torcal de Antequera,
these shales are seen to dip under the series of white and red marbles which constitute the upper part of this formation.

In these shales I have not found a single fossil, therefore I am
unable to decide whether they form part of the series of white and
red marbles or if they form another distinct part of the Jurassic
formation. Nevertheless in the Puerto de las Palomas, between
Villaluenga and Grazalema, the contact between these two deposits
may be observed, and they are seen to pass from one to the other
through insensible gradations.

The upper marbles have also a very considerable thickness and
their character are very similar every where: white and red marbles,
sometimes extremely finely grained, and which are then employed
in the different towns of Andalusia as ornamental marbles.

In this Province the fossils in this part of the formation are
not very abundant, still near Prado de Rey I have seen a great
abundance of small apthycus, and from near Villaluenga I have
seen a large specimen of the Ammonites Achilles, a fossil which
has also been found near Antequera by M. Orueta.

At Prado de Rey and Benamahoma these marbles are seen at
the base of the third group.

This group is of the greatest interest. It is formed by a powerful
aggregate of bluish gray and white marly limestones, extremely
rich in organic remains, though generally in an indifferent state of
preservation.

In some places at the base of this marly limestone, a very
thick deposit of white marble, very similar petrologically considered
to the Stramberg marbles, is found.

Where this marble is wanting at the base of the formation, a
series of marly limestones, of a bluish gray colour are seen in its
stead, the bluish tint of which is gradually lost till the upper part
of the deposit is constituted by a yellowish white marl extremely
rich in organic remains.

These white marls in the Berrueco, Jigonza and other places
pass directly to the white marbles, and then the series of blue limestones which are so powerful near Alcala, Prado de Rey etc. are
apparently wanting.

The places where I have seen these white marbles are Jigonza near Paterna, at the Peñas de Armes in the Sierra del Algibe, La Granja near Medina and the Berrueco near Chiclana, besides other small patches in different parts of the Province.

In the upper part of the Berrueco, the white marls are found with Ammonites Subfimbriatus and other fossils, which prove them to belong to the inferior Neocomian, Below these marls, are found the series of white marbles, which can be seen exposed more than eighty meters in vertical height without any signs of dis-appearing.

These marbles are frequently oolitic, and frequently also have quite a litographicstone structure. Their colour changes from white to yellowish white. A great quantity of organic remains are found in these marbles, generally brachiopods, and of which M. Hebert has determined the following: Rhynconella Suessi. Rh. Spattica, Rh. Striatoplicata, Rh. Trilobata, Rh. Astierriana, Terebratula Ebrodunensis, Ter Magadiformis, Ter Mitis. Ter Cataphracta.

In the white as well as in part at least of the blue marls of the rest of the Province the Terebratula Janitor is abundantly found accompanied by the following fossils.

Ammonites Fimbriatus, Am. Rouyanus, Am. Astierrianus, Am. Grasianus, Am. Asperrimus, Am. Ptychoichus, Am. Occita-nicus, Crioceras Duvalii, Terebratulu Bouei.

Are the totality of these deposits Neocomian, as the white marls specially seem to indicate, or are the white marbles and perhaps the inferior blue marls, representatives of the so hotly controverted Thithonic horizon and which form with the red marbles an uninterrupted whole?

I dare not arrive at any definite conclusion in this matter and leave the question open to other observers, who better qualified than myself may venture to solve this problem.

In Conil and quite close to the sulphur deposits a small patch of the Cretaceous formation is found, extremely rich in small fer-ruginous Ammonites, of which the above mentioned M. Hebert has determined the following: Am. Striatosulcatus, Am. Guettardi, Am. Belus, Am. Duvalianus, Am. Asperrimus (v), Am. Deshayesi, Am. Picturatus Am. Dyphillus.

DESCRIPTION OF THE EOCENE AND MIOCENE
DEPOSITS.

The Tertiary deposits of this Province, occupy a very considerable extent of ground.

This formation forms three great groups, which seem to represent the Eocene, Miocene and Pliocene deposits of Northern Europe.

The first group is composed of a calcareous deposit, poor in fossils with the exception of nummulites, alternating in some places with more or less indurated clays and marls.

The second is formed by a great thickness of sandstones, marls and calcareous conglomerate, covered by the third group composed of incoherent sands and calcareous conglomerate, very rich in organic remains. I colour the two inferior deposits with the same tint in the map, as they form an aggregate very difficult to separate, not so much through the similarity of their petrological characters as on account of the numerous outcrops of the inferior deposits through the strata of the higher.

The lower deposits however occupy in the southern part of the Province nearly the whole of the depression of the Janda Lake, as well as the low ground between Medina and Alcala and a very considerable portion of the valleys of the rivers Palmones and Guadiaro, whilst the summits of the adjoining Sierras are formed by the upper sandstones.

These two great groups have a great similarity to the Tertiary rocks of Southern Europe. The inferior part of the formation seems to correspond to the Nummulitic limestone, and the other at least in its lower part, seems equivalent to the Flysh and Macigno.

The totality of these deposits, when petrologically considered, form two very distinct regions.

In the North of the Province the lower part is formed of an extremely soft white marly limestone, and the upper one of another great thickness of clays and marls.

In the South the inferior deposits are formed of alternating layers of compact limestone with more or less indurated clays, and superposed to this very potent beds of sandstones completely barren in organic remains. Towards the western part of the Province these sandstones terminate by a thick deposit of calcareous conglomerate rich in organic remains, though generally in fragments.

These two regions may be divided aproximately by a line which in a N. E. direction would touch the Province in the vicinity of Cape Roche and pass between Villamartin and Prado de Rey.

The white marly limestone which forms the base of the Tertiary deposits in the North of the Province are of considerable thickness, and though not very frequently layers are interposed within them which are a perfect conglomerate of Nummulites.

The excavated valley formed by the Salado river, which from the Salineta de Guerra flows into the Zurraque 12 kilometers S. E. of Port Royal, is one of the places where these alternating layers can be best observed.

The limestone is extremely shally in some places and then the planes of stratification are extremely difficult to recognize. In the small outcrop of this deposit to the E. N. E. of Port Royal the strata is crossed in every direction by polished surfaces of friction, and where this has taken place the carbonate of lime has cristalized within the rock to a depth of more than five milimeters.

The great thickness of these deposits can be observed with the greatest advantage in their contact with the Neocomian strata of the Sierra del Valle near the Venta of that name and there its total thickness cannot be reckoned at less than 500 meters.

The marly strata in this place are covered by a siliceous limestone, which occupies the whole of this intermediate region between the northern marls and the southern sandstones. In this deposit I have not found a single fossil, but taking into account the absence of both the marls and the sandstones of the upper deposit in this region; I consider it, though with reserve, as their equivalent.

The strata of this upper part of the deposits are constituted by a series of ash gray and bluish gray marls very poor in fossils, though teeth of Squalus carcareus are frequently met with.

Their thickness is very considerable, as it can be seen by following the cuttings in the high roads from Medina and Jerez to Arcos and Bornos. From about three or four miles before Arcos to about one mile further on the road to Bornos, the whole of the Tertiary series can be observed, from the white Nummulitic marls to the Pliocene sands covered by the diluvium.

This marly formation, which towards the N. W. of the Province becomes nearly a pure clay, does not posses the equality of characters which characterizes the sandstones of the south of the Province, the synchronism of which, at least in part, I consider highly probable.

From the hills of Espera to the Sierras Rabita and Asnar there exists a great thickness of a calcareous conglomerate which abounds in large oysters and pectens as well as other Miocene fossils.

This deposit has a great similarity to the middle Tertiaries of the valley of the Guadalquivir and of which they seem contemporaneous. In somes places of the hills of Espera this conglomerate acquires a semi cristaline appearance, and is occasionally deeply tinted by red peroxide of iron, which gives to the rock a much older appearance than that which corresponds to the Miocene strata.

The hilly tract of ground between Jerez and Puerto is constituted at its base by a soft white limestone literally filled with Nummulites. This rock gradually becomes more and more sandy till the upper part of the hills are formed of a sandstone with calcareous cement formed of small fragments of shells and corals and small grains of hyaline quartz, known under the name of Piedra franca del Puerto de Santa Maria.

In the southern portion of the Province the characters of the Tertiary deposits are quite different to those already described.

The lower part of the Tertiary desposits in this region is represented either by shally micaceous clay, or by a series of alternating beds of clay and limestone, or by a great predominance of this substance.

In the extreme southern limits of the Province, particularly in all the tract of ground between Tarifa and Algeciras, is where the alternating layers of clays and limestones can be best observed.

In this place these deposits are formed by a succession of layers of limestone, which vary in their thickness from one centimeter to two or more decimeters, separated by thin beds of clay which vary in tint from red to green blue or yellow and possessing always a more or less variegated colour.

The limestones are always extremely compact and always more or less siliceous. They posses a semi cristaline structure and cement small green grains of glauconia.

These green grains of glauconia seem to be characteristic of all the limestones of this part of the formation, and even in the white marls of the North of the Province this same mineral is seen ✦ filling the tests of the Nummulites at the Salineta de Guerra.

The colour of these limestone layers is bluish gray sometimes yellow veined.

Frequently they possess a brechiform structure and they cement small fragments from the Secondary deposits.

Nummulites are difficult to be met with in this part of the formation owing to the cristaline state of the rock; nevertheless near Tarifa I have seen them in great abundance and tolerably well preserved.

Though I have seen no other organic remains except the above mentioned Nummulites, still in some of the flags proceeding from this formation, and which are employed as paving stones at Cadiz, I have seen some which are a perfect conglomerate of shells.

Between Algeciras and Los Barrios the limestones become scarcer, and in their stead appear indurated shally micaceous clays.

The colour of these clays is a light gray with a touch of yellowish green, and in some places they are extremely altered and the shales are reduced to a deep reddish purple clay. Small isolated patches of the primitive clays frequently outcrop in the midst of these clays.

A similar phenomenon is seen in other parts of the Province, especially near the town of Jimena on the road to Gaucin, between Alcala and Casas Viejas and between Medina and Chiclana, as well as in many other places; and this partial decompo-

sition is found always in strict correspondance with the anticlinal
axis of the folds.

With the exception of these two deposits of shales and alternating beds of clays and limestones; limestones always alternating
with more or less thick layers of clay, constitute the rest of the
inferior Tertiary deposits of this region.

These limestones occupy the lower part of all the valleys and
ravines where the upper sandstones have been denuded, and
almost exclusively form the low tract of ground between the hills
of Medina and those of Alcala.

Similarly to the Tarifa flags these limestones also form slabs
though of a greater thickness as a rule.

Their colour is generally of a light yellowish gray and they
cement the same green grains of glauconia.

The rock is at times a perfect conglomerate of nummulites,
which are perfectly recognizable, as it does not possess the cristaline structure to such a degree as the limestones near the straits.

Frequently veins and nodules of flint are met with in all these
limestones.

This rock rarely ontcrops in large masses. They generally
form rounded hills covered from their base to their summit with
angular fragments of the limestone flags, and sometimes in such
quantity that they are a real impediment in going over the land,
especially between Paterna and Alcala.

When all these masses of angular fragments of rock are seen,
sometimes partially buried in the soil, and others completely superposed and huddled together in utter confusion on the summits
of the hills, as if they had been carried there from a higher level, we
are at a loss for a theory to explain such an extraordinary phenomenon; but when the rocks are seen in situ it is easily accounted
for by the fractured state of the limestones flags, and by the
running waters carrying away the thin beds of clay which separate
the different layers and which thus leave the limestone fragments
heaped upon each other in perfect confusion.

The upper part of this formation or the Miocene deposits are
represented in this region by a very powerful deposit of sandstones,
which as Mr. Smith says in his Geology of Gibraltar, might very

well be taken in some places for equivalent to the Millstone grit of the Carboniferous period.

Their colour is a light yellowish brown and they are formed by a fine grained sand, though sometimes the size of the grains augment and become as large as small almonds. Frequently these beds, as for instance between Medina and Casas Viejas, may be considered almost a pudding stone.

Sometimes the sand is formed of nearly hyaline quartz and the country then, as it happens between Medina and Torre Estrella, is of a dazzling whiteness.

At other places the sandstones are coloured a vivid red by anhydrous peroxide of iron, as is specially the case near the Casas del Castaño, where the rock assumes an extremely old· appearance.

In the hills of Medina, specially towards Paterna, this sandstone alternates with thin layers of plastic clay. It is very remarkable to observe the gradual transition which takes place between the Southern sandstones and the Northern marls and clays in all this region down to Cape Trafalgar, and where this passage can be best examined is between the Altos de Patria and Veger.

This gradual transition is in my judgement one of the facts which principally tend to establish the equivalence of the upper sandstones and marls.

This assumption is further confirmed on approaching the mass of Secondary limestones of the Sierra, on both sides of which the Tertiary deposits acquire totally different characters, whilst the deposits of the intermediate zone appear to have been formed in a much shallower sea than that in which the other parts of the Tertiary formation were deposited.

In my judgement the mass of Jurassic limestones formed during the Tertiary epoch a succession of shoals or an archipelago which greatly influenced ths deposits of that sea.

The sandstones of the south of the Province are completely barren in organic remains, and only in the calcareous conglomerate which terminates this deposit towards Medina and Veger are some oysters and pectens found though generally in fragments.

Their thickness is very considerable and together with the

inferior deposits form a most powerful series of Tertiary strata.

The summits of the Sierra del Algibe are formed of this sandstone, and though the summits must have been considerably denuded, a fair notion of its thickness can here be obtained.

The difference of level between the outcrop of the Neocomian rocks, in their contact with the Nummulitic limestones in the Puerto de las Palomas and the summit of the Picacho, is more than 700 meters, but as the horizontal distance between the outcrop of the Neocomian rocks and the Picacho is considerable, and the strata dip rapidly to the N. W., the thickness must naturally be still greater and it must be reckoned at not less than one thousand meters.

In the Sierra de Retin, when this rock is desintegrated through apparently atmospherical influences, the resulting sand takes a vivid red tint.

This passage of the iron to its state of anhydrous peroxide is in some places very remarkable, owing to the considerable extent of ground it occupies; and when superficially observed it might be mistaken for the diluvial deposits, which as it will be seen in the sequel possess a very similar character.

DESCRIPTION OF THE PLIOCENE AND RECENT
DEPOSITS.

The study of the Pliocene and Postpliocene deposits are highly interesting in this Province, and perhaps may help us in the solution of more than one complicated problem.

The City of Cadiz is built on an important Pliocene formation. These deposits are always more or less arenaceous and repose on the Miocene clays.

This was seen when the foundations for the fortifications on the southern beach were constructed, as well as when some years ago works were executed for the construction of an artesian well. The place where these deposits can be best examined is the low cliff formed by the breakers in the southern beach.

This cliff follows the direction of the coast during some 900 meters describing an arc of a circle, the centre of which is in the sea.

The strata on their first outcrop near the fortifications dip 20 degees to the S. E. whilst they are nearly horizontal when they are lost under the sands of the beach, the Miocene clays near the Bull ring forming apparently an anticlinal axis.

The total thickness of these deposits in Cadiz, if the data I have employed are exact, cannot be reckoned at less than 300 meters.

The fossil which characterizes the whole of this formation is the Pecten Jacobeus, which is accompanied either in one or the other of its different strata by the Pecten Cristatus, P. Pixidatus, P. Scabrellus, P. Benedictus, P. Coarctatus, P. Varius, Lima Inflata, Ostrea Edulis, and Ostrea Pseudoedulis.

As seen in section N.° 2 the first strata that appears is a fine marly sand with impresions of small shells in a very inferior state of preservation. This marly sand is followed by incoherent sands with alternating layers and nodules of carbonate of lime extremely abundant in fossils, amongst them the Pectens Jacobeus, Pixidatus, Scabrellus and Ostrea Edulis.

Overlaying these sands are found about two meters in thickness of a marly sand very similar to that seen at the first outcrop of the formation with the same impressions of shells and occasionally fine specimens of Pecten Cristatus.

Above these marly sands a considerable thickness of a blue and yellow marl relatively poor in fossils is met with, overlapped by another great thickness of incoherent sands extremely abundant in organic remains, amongst which numerous specimens of the Lima Inflata are found.

Following these sands a hard conglomerate of oysters and Pectens appears, which passes to another conglomerate of extremely different characters.

The inferior deposit is exclusively formed of sand and the above mentioned organic remains, whilst the uppermost deposit is composed of shells frequently in fragments and united to them by calcareous cement a great quantity of rolled pebbles, generally quarzites.

It is a most important fact to observe that, in conjunction with the quarzites and other rocks, innumerable fragments of the layers and nodules of carbonate of lime, which constitute part of this very same formation, are found.

This fact establishes the gradual upheaval of these strata, for it is evident that whilst the Pliocene period had not yet fully terminated, its deposits had been sufficiently upheaved above the sea to be battered by its waves, and that the ruins of these deposits constitute a portion of the entire series which we distinguish under the name of Pliocene.

On observing the strict correspondance which exists between the upheaval of these deposits and the folds which have contorted the strata of the Province, it is natural to conclude that they are the result of one of those violent and sudden disturbances which we are generally so prone to accept; but the inferences we are bound to admit from this fact show how extremely cautious we must be with regard to the duration of some of the most violent disturbances of our globe.

This like many other profound commotions observed in our planet and which we refer to a tragic and violent cataclysm, which at a given moment may have afflicted the inhabitants of this globe, may perhaps be only the sum of a slow and gradual disturbance, which may have required periods of enormous magnitude for ist realization, and may have passed quite unperceived by the beings then peopling the earth.

To this conglomerate there follows about two meters in thick ness of alternating layers of clay and white chalk, and the whole is covered by what appears to be a beach deposit of large rolled pebbles and sand, which near the cemetery possesses a thickness in some places of four meters. This is the last Pliocene strata of Cadiz.

Covering the whole of this formation, and in unconformable stratification, there exists a sandy clay of a vivid red colour which covers a very considerable portion of Andalusia.

This diluvial deposit I will describe hereafter.

At the base of the cliff I have described, and specially in the place named Punta del Blanco, there is found a conglomerate of large stones, sand and organic remains frequently in fragments, amongst them the Cardium Edulis, resting unconformably on the Pliocene beds.

As easily seen in section N.º 3, besides other reasons which will appear hereafter, this conglomerate appears to be subsequent to the diluvial deposit.

It occupies a very considerable extent of ground, stretching in patches of more or less importance from the above mentioned Punta del Blanco to the Promontory of San Sebastian. Subsequently to its deposit this formation has been slightly upheaved, as part of it is at a higher level than the highest tides of the present time.

In the rest of the Province the Pliocene deposits present similar characters to those, which they possess in the Isla Gaditana. Incoherent sands and more or less sandy marls at the base and conglomerates in its upper part, are the distinguishing characters of the Pliocene strata in this region.

The thickness of this conglomerate is considerably greater in some places than what it attains in the Cadiz fallaise. At Port Royal for instance it attains nearly twenty meters.

These deposits constitute a belt bordering the present coast and hardly ever penetrate further inland than ten to twelve kilometers.

Nevertheless, between Paterna and Alcala, I have seen in a small patch of incoherent sands, numerous specimens of the Pecten Scabrellus, and it is very probable that the Pliocene deposits may exist covered by the diluvium over the calcareous conglomerate of the Mesa de Casas Viejas, similarly to what happens in the Altos de Patria and other eminences in the vicinity of Veger·

Besides this, in the valley of the Guadalete there are extensive tracts of ground covered by the Pliocene deposits, and this shows that the Pliocene sea, on that side at least, reached further inland than Arcos.

This town is built on a potent deposit of incoherent sands and layers of carbonate of lime, which in the celebrated Tajo are cut vertically to a depth of more than 100 meters.

Organic remains are rare in the lower parts of this sandy deposit, but at a higher level and more than 200 meters above the sea, especially in the road to Bornos, a large amount of fossils are found, amongst them the Pectens Scabrellus, Cristatus and Pixidatus.

In all the tract of comparatively level ground between Arcos and Jerez, frequent signs are observed which prove that the remains of this formation are more numerous than what is marked on the chart, but the want of natural or artificial sections, have not allowed me to mark their presence with any degree of certainty.

At the mouth of the Guadalquivir in the headland where the Castillo del Espiritu Santo is built, and close to Sanlucar there exists a most interesting section of the Pliocene formation in its contact with the Miocene clays, which appear to form an anticlinal axis.

In the alternating beds of calcareous conglomerate with clays and sands which constitute the Pliocene strata in this place are found an extraordinary abundance of organic remains, amongst which M. Bayan has determined the following: Pecten Benedictus, Cardium Hians, Cardium Ciliare, Solen Bordugalensis, Corbula Striata, Ostrea Boblayé, Turritella Vermicularis, Natica Josephine (vec).

Covering the whole of this formation to the depth of three or four meters there exists a course ferruginous sand, in which M. Lujan affirms having found remains of the Bos Aurox.

Besides the modern deposits of the Cadiz Caleta and the diluvium there exist some most interesting recent deposits. One of them is the mighty clay deposit which constitutes the whole of the level tract of ground near Cadíz bay. These clays are evidently the sediments deposited by the different rivers which flow into the bay, and if it were not for the current which is established by the Santi Petri channel, owing to the difference of hour in the tides of the Ocean and those at the bottom of the Bay, these sediments would in a very short period completely block up this fine harbour, which notwithstanding this splendid system of drainage, is gradually diminishing in depth.

In the valley of the Guadalete, and especially between the Pasada del Alamillo and the Pedrosa, there exist some very important alluvial deposits, formed of blocks and pebbles of considerable size, which at the base of the Sierras de las Cabras and Alajar near the banks of the Majaceite, are firmly cemented by carbonate of lime, forming highly compact travertines. At the base of the mountains near Algeciras I have also observed great deposits of large rolled blocks, but in this case without the slightest cement.

In the upper part of the Mesa de Meca there exists a succession of sand hills extremely remarkable. Cape Trafalgar forms an elevated headland, of about 170 meters above the sea, which terminates by a rapid talus in the beach.

The southwest winds blow with great force near this Cape, and carry the sands of the beach to the highest part of the promontory, dispersing them in the elevated plateau in a series of hillocks, which give to this part of the country, as its name implies, a great similarity to the vicinity of the Holy city of the Prophet.

On the upper part of the talus, the calcareous conglomerate protrudes. The wind does not allow the sand to rest here, and owing to the constant friction of the grains of sand on the rock, it is as smoothly polished as if it had been artificially effected. Also in the vecinity of Port St. Mary's there exist a succession of sand hillocks, from ten to twelve meters high, but which do not penetrate to any great distance inland.

When speaking of the Cadiz Pliocene deposits, I stated that the diluvium covered the whole of the island in unconformable stratification with the Pliocene formation.

This deposit covers a considerable portion af the Province, and testifies to the profound disturbances which this part of the continent has suffered in a relatively modern epoch.

Generally this deposit does not cover the actual depressions of the ground, but on the contrary it occupies a relatively high level, frequently the summits of small parallelograms which exist between the longitudinal valleys, which as a rule follow what were convexities of the folds and the great transversal valleys which cut the Province form one extreme to the other.

During this epoch the waters evidently ran over the troughs of the folds, which were the valleys at that time and are now the summits of the hills; the erosions not having then been sufficient to degrade to their present level the newly folded strata, nor had the series of fractures which fissured the country at right angles to the direction of these folds yet taken place, and which have so essentially changed the orographical structure of this district.

One of the best examples where the magnitude of the erosions which have taken place after the diluvial epoch may be seen, is in the vicinity of Arcos.

The River Guadalete between this town and Bornos breaks through the series of hills named Sierras del Calvario and Santiscar, on the summits of which the diluvium is found perfectly well characterized; and as it can be seen in section N.º 5 there exists a difference of level of more than 200 meters, which can only be accounted for through erosions in a posterior epoch to the diluvial deposit.

A similar phenomenon is seen in the Altos de Patria between Conil and Veger, as seen in section N.º 6.

The diluvium crowns the summits of these heights at 170 meters above the sea, while in the lowest parts of the valley of the River Salado de Conil, which runs at only 15 meters above the sea and quite close to an outcrop of ophite, not the slightest traces of diluvial deposits exist.

The characteristics of this deposit are very similar everywhere, and consist of a vivid red sandy clay without the least appearance of stratification or cement, accompanied by innumerable pebbles, generally of the size of walnuts, but sometimes as large as oranges.

A problem of very great importance is raised through the appearance of these pebbles on the western coast of the Province.

From the south of Cape Trafalgar to the Punta Candor, as well as also between San Roque and the Convent of the Almorayma, the pebbles which accompany this deposit are well nigh exclusively quarzites whilst those of the interior of the Province are replaced by others of a different nature.

It is difficult to account from whence these pebbles are derived, as this rock does not exist in the Province.

Do they proceed from the Province of Malaga when the orographical structure of the country was different to what it is at present?

How then does it happen that this rock is not found in the deposits nearest to that Province, but on the contrary their frequency augments the nearer the coast, and in a direct ratio to the increase of distance from that supposed focus?

Do they proceed from the Sierra Morena? It is difficult to accept this conclusion through the absence of those pebbles in the North of the Province, through which they ought, necessarily to have passed before reaching the southern part, and after traversing the valley of the Guadalquivir.

This, added to the many artificial disturbances which would be required to explain the difference of the levels on which these deposits are found, make me greatly doubt this hypothesis.

Do they perchance proceed from lands to the west, which have disappeared in consequence of the last disturbance which in a -post diluvial epoch has so profoundly disturbed this part of the European continent?

I am perhaps broaching one of the most complex geological problems, but on considering the number of independant facts which through different channels tend to confirm this supposition, I cannot refrain from taking it into account.

On observing the series of heights which stretch from the banks of the Guadiaro to the coast of the Atlantic, studying at the same time their intimate structure; and observing the diluvium crowning the summits of the litoral hills, we are forcibly struck with the notion that there have existed territories which might have been the prolongation of this series of mountains, which terminate so abruptly on the shores of the Atlantic.

Moreover, though the Altos de Patria are from ten to twelve kilometers nearer the coast than the Mesa de Casas Viejas, the diluvium reposes here at a higher level; the difference attaining 90 meters, a fact which suggests the probability that the waters in this place ran from the coast inland.

In the preceeding orographical description, I have pointed out the series of valleys of fractures which at right angles to the folds disconnect these series of hills, and which as it happens with the one nearest to the coast where the Janda lake is formed show a difference of level of more than 700 meters, proclaiming how profoundly this part of the country has been affected by this modern disturbance.

If we add these facts to the recentness of the epoch when the Great Desert of Sahara was part of a great sea, when in all probability the Great Atlas Mountains and the actual Morocco were separated from the Continent of Africa.

If we also take into account the great freshwater lakes of the Peninsula, which seem to indicate the existance of a larger extent of territory than the present, at least during the Miocene epoch, which would explain the supply of these lakes. If we consider also the similarity of the faunas and floras of Southern Europe and Northern Africa we have a large body of facts, which all tend to support the belief in the existance of a larger tract of territory to the west; and which at a not remote period connected the actual Morocco with the Iberian Peninsula, the union of which is abundantly testified by what exists on both sides of the straits of Gibraltar.

Probably the series of transverse fractures which are found in this Province have been the consequence of the lever motion and necessary rupture, which this part of the Earth experienced when a not insignificant part perhaps of that ancient territory disappeared beneath the sea level.

It is however premature to enter fully into this interesting question which I have only hinted at, so as to call the attention of observers towards so important a fact, which might perhaps explain the tradition which in remote historical times yet prevailed amongst the Egyptian priests regarding the disappearance of the famous Atlantida.

DESCRIPTION OF THE ERUPTIVE ROCKS AND
GYPSIFEROUS DEPOSITS.

Great importance is attached to the study of the gypsiferous deposits of this Province, for though their petrological characters as well as their appearing frequently superimposed by Jurassic deposits, might induce us to consider them as Triassic, their association with other stratified rocks, the organic remains which though sparingly are found within their strata, and numerous other facts, raise serious doubts as to whether or not they should be so considered. I am more inclined to consider these deposits as the result of a profound epigenesis which has taken place since the Miocene epoch, than to consider them as any especially stratified deposit.

These gypsiferous rocks form a broad belt which traverse the entire Province in a W. S. W. to E. N. E. direction to the North of a line which would unite the Pico del Algibe with Cape Trafalgar.

The limits I give to this formation are somewhat arbitrary, for it is frequently observed that whilst the base of a hill is formed of gypsum or dolomite, its summit is constituted by a more or less important patch of any of the different stratified deposits of this Province. These limits therefore only indicate the places where epigenic action has more or less actively taken place.

The patches of this formation outcrop in the midst of all the geological strata of this Province. At Puerto Real and Espera they are found in contact with the middle Tertiaries, whilst at Paterna, Medina and the Salineta de Guerra they outcrop amidst the inferior deposits.

Not only in the Tertiary deposits does this anomaly take place. In the Berrueco, La Granja and Jigonza they are found in contact with the Neocomian strata. In Prado de Rey and El Bosque they appear under the red Jurassic marbles, whilst in Benamahoma and Ubrique they protrude from under the Liassic limestones, or beneath the calcareous shales which constitute the base of this formation.

These deposits are invariably found in strict correspondence with the anticlinal axis of the folds which have disturbed the strata of all this region, and which are in some places most violently disturbed.

Section N.º 8 will give an idea of the extraordinary contortions which they have experienced.

'They are accompanied by an eruptive rock which in some places is extremely abundant.

The characters of this rock are very variable. Sometimes they are eminently massive and compact and might be taken for a basalt, and at others they show a perfect cristalline structure; but as a rule their cristalline structure is very obscure.

Their colour changes from a grayish green to a dark green or black; or as it happens in their outcrop to the S. W. of Alcala, in a perfectly cristalline white felspar, ill defined cristals of probably black pyroxene are seen.

All these rocks treated by boiling hidrocloric acid loose from 5 to 15 % of their weight. In the solution rather considerable portions of iron and of magnesia are found.

These rocks seem to be formed of a triclinic felspar and pyroxene, besides a soluble silicate of magnesia, which tends to give to the rock that appearance of obscure cristallization it possesses, for when fragments are boiled in hidrocloric acid, and then in a solution of potash to disolve the adhering gelatinous silica, their crystalline structure is then perfectly well seen.

These rocks are always more or less magnetic, and follow the needle even in tolerably large pieces. Small particles of pyrites are frequently found in their mass. Their density is very considerable, and varies from 2, 8 to 3, 1.

In some places they are profoundly decomposed, and when this takes place, the rock is frequently traversed by small veins and concretions of specular iron.

One of the places where this altered state of the rock can be best observed, is in two of the three outcrops which are to be found in the road which leads from the Berrueco to Medina, especially in that nearest to this town, where the rock is reduced to a fine sand.

As these rocks are similar in characters, and have appeared probably at the same recent period as the Ophites of the Pyrenees. To avoid the inconvenience of introducing unnecessarily a new name, I will distinguish them as such, though perhaps they may not be identical.

The outcroppings of these rocks are very frequent; and especially so between Medina and Chiclana, where I have seen seventeen, and this number, I doubt not, may be only a small fraction of what really exists, for as they form only small protuberances in the lowest part of the valleys and ravines, it is a difficult task to observe them.

As a rule they are of small dimensions; yet sometimes they are of considerable size. One of the most remarkable outcrops for its size is the one seen to the North of the Berrueco near the Pozo del Hierro, which runs parallel to the major axis of this elliptical hill during nearly the whole of its length.

Another outcrop, remarkable also for its size, is the one seen near the town of El Bosque on the road to Arcos. This outcrop is a rounded hill of about six-hundred meters in diameter and one hundred meters high.

These ophites as a rule form rounded hills covered by angular fragments of the same rock. Nevertheless they sometimes have a very extraordinary appearance; as is the case near the River Almendron between Puerto Real and Medina, where a sharply defined cone of this rock may be seen.

On the summit of this cone, the peculiarity which these rocks posses of breaking in polyhedrical fragments is highly exaggerated; and similarly to what Mr. Darwin has observed in the outcrops of Greenstone of South America, the higher part of the cone is composed of large fragments of this rock huddled over each other in complete confusion.

Another outcrop extremely remarkable for its form, is the horn shaped rock seen in the middle of the plain near the springs of Tempul.

Between the Berrueco and Medina there is another peculiar outcrop not so on acconnt of its form but through its situation.

In the centre of a small round plain of about five hundred meters diameter a small protuberance of ophite is seen, which raises over it scarcely more than ten or twelve meters.

These circular spaces are frequently seen in the gypsiferous formation, and at first sight they might be considered ancient craters.

However different the deposits which accompany these outcroppings of ophites may be in their composition, they always possess the same common character, as for instance the variegated colour of the clays and the cellular structure of the limestones.

When this formation acquires its normal development its characters are very similar everywhere.

In this case the strata of this formation are formed of great masses of gypsum, sometimes alternating and others mixed together with variegated clays and dolomites.

These dolomites are sometimes compact and others extremely cellular, and their colour changes from ash gray to nearly black.

The structure of these dolomites is frequently very shally.

Alternating with these rocks, beds of sandstones are sometimes seen, generally of a deep red colour, and small particles of mica are seen between the planes of clivage.

Gypsums sometimes acquire considerable thickness, and to the S. E. of La Granja on the banks of the Rio del Alamo there are hills, more than one hundred meters higher than the bed of the river totally formed of this rock.

Stratification cannot be recognised in these gypsum rocks, which generally form irregular masses, frequently of a brechiform structure, cementing large fragments of clays and dolomites within their mass.

The clays and gypsums are sometimes literally full of crystals of bipyramidal quartz. Between Puerto Real and Medina I have seen red gypsums cementing red Hyacinths of Compostella and near Chiclana I have seen black gypsums cementing black crystals of bipyramidal quartz.

These crystals acquire sometimes very considerable dimensions, and near Medina I have seen pyramids of more than two centimeters at their base.

The colour of the gypsums frequently change, but as a rule red and black are the predominant tints. Sometimes, though rarely, they are perfectly hyaline.

In the place named Barrancos de Puerto Real I have seen alternating layers of gypsums and magnesite.

This substance is in so intimate connextion with the gypsum, that veins and ramifications of this last mineral traverses it in all directions.

In this same place another very interesting phenomenon can also be observed, which however is frequently seen in other parts, of this Province.

It is the brechiform state of the dolomites near their contact with the ophites. The rock is reduced to minute fragments, but instead of falling to pieces, no particle of cement being observable, the rock adheres together as if the fragments of this species of breccia had been soldered together through the great pressures which it seems to have experienced.

At about 3 kilometers E. N. E. of Chiclana there exists an outcrop of ophite, which as seen in section N.º 9, has lifted a block of limestone which besides having been transformed into a crystalline dolomite, is full of small cells filled with clay of a light green colour.

Crystalline dolomites are also frequently seen near the contact of the ophites, but they rarely extend to any great distance.

I have already referred to the state of decomposition in which the Nummulitic shales are found at Jimena, los Barrios etc., and this phenomenon seems to be in strict correspondance to the one I am describing.

Between Algar and Ubrique and to the S. E. of Alcala and many other places the Nummulitic formation is highly impregnated with peroxide of manganese, whilst near Medina I have seen limestones of the same formation with all its fissures filled with small concretions of opal.

The sulphur deposits seem also intimately connected with all these semi-volcanic actions. Those of Conil are widely known owing to the fine specimens of crystallized sulphur they produce.

The really important deposits of the Province, however, are those of Arcos where, as seen in section N.º 7, the Tertiary clays are impregnated by the sulphur in apparently very strict correspondence with the gypsiferous deposits which at a short distance are seen on the banks of the Salado de Espera.

The mud volcanoes observed in this region seem also intimately connected with this phenomenon.

In Conil there are a great number of these small cones now extinct, but according to M. Delanoue, at Moron in the Province of Seville many of them are still in activity.

In the only other part of the Province where I have seen these mud volcanoes in activity is near the Peña Arpada between Paterna and Alcala.

About 300 meters from the outcrop of ophite at the base of that rock there existed in May 1870 a very perfect, though small mud volcano.

This truncated cone was about two meters high and about four meters in diameter at its base. It was formed of a fine black mud, and at its upper part there existed a small pool of water from whence gas bubbles with a strong smell of sulphurretted hydrogen were constantly disengaged.

The water was so highly saturated with Chloride of Sodium that the salt crystallized on the slopes of the cone and gave it the appearance of a heap of snow.

This emanation of gases is frequently observed, but not from cones: it generally takes place from the river beds.

In the Arroyo del Almendron, about two kilometers to the east of the Berrueco, large tracts of the bed of the river are formed of a fine black mud, from which there is an abundant disengagement of sulphurous gases.

In the Salineta de Guerra I have likewise observed a similar phenomenon; but here, instead of the mud being of a black colour, it had a yellowish red tint, and small mud protuberances of the most varied colours covered the entire bed of the river; whilst irregular bubbles of gases were constantly disengaged from the centre of these small protuberances.

In these gases there was not a trace of Sulphuretted hydrogen. This might have been a priori inferred, as these clays would otherwise have lost their varied tints. Owing to the strong wind then blowing I could not ascertain whether the gases were inflammable or not. I observed this phenomenon in May 1871, but in the following October it had completely disappeared.

Near a small rivulet, which flows into the Almendron, there exists a sulphurous spring which mixes its waters with those of this small rivulet, when its bed is covered by a white loam, which after being dried and heated in a close tube gives an abundant disengagement of Sulphuretted hydrogen and a sublimate of sulphur, leaving a black carbonaceous residue.

Salt springs are also extremely abundant in all this region, and in Prado de Rey extensive salt pans are being worked since a very remote time.

Sulphuretted springs are numerous also; and some, as for instance Fuente Amarga and Braque in Chiclana and Jigonza near Paterna are employed as medicinal waters.

After having described some of the most important characters which these deposits possess, I will now describe some of those cases whieh will help to enlighten us as to the true horizon where this formation ought to be placed.

In Chiclana to the S. W. of the town there exists a small hill known as Santa Ana.

This hill is formed of an extremely remarkable limestone.

It is very compact and silicious, and at some places to such a degree, that it is literally a sandstone with calcareous cement.

At other times the rock is an extremely homogenous limestone and cements within its mass small particles of mica. A considerable quantity of magnesía enters also into the composition of this rock, and it possesses all the characters of a dolomite. It is full of cavities which are covered with concretions of carbonate of lime, and sometimes small geodes of arragonite.

Its colour varies from nearly white or yellowish white to a dark blue.

This deposit is extremely rich in fossils, of which however only the casts are preserved. Their determination is extremely difficult, but they are undoubtedly Tertiary, and M. Verneuil considered a Polyp found here as closely related to the Caryophillia Truncata of the Nummulitic period. This deposit rests on the white Nummulitic marls, as seen in section N.º 12.

The strata between the Santa Ana Hill and the Baths of Fuente Amarga is doubly folded, and in the anticlinal axis of the fold nearest to Santa Ana, variegated marls and gypsum are seen to pass to the white Nummulitic marls in the cuttings of the road which leads from Chiclana to these baths.

After passing this fold in the strata and close to a windmill, at about a kilometer before reaching the Baths, the same compact magnesian limestone as is seen at Santa Ana is found and which at the upper part of the hill has those identical characters which indicate a partial metamorphic state.

At a short distance from the summit of the hill in the cuttings of the road this metamorphic state is still more pronounced. The rock gradually acquires a darker colour; its structure becomes extremely compact and in some places almost lithographic.

Besides this, the cast, of the fossils become more and more indistinct, and at the same time finely defined crytals of bipyramidal quartz are seen firmly inbedded in the rock. Gradually these crystals augment in size and quantity, and an inmense number of small hexagonal prims of Aragonite also appear firmly imbedded in the rock, which then has the appearance of a species of porphyr. Shortly after these limestones become cellular and gradually pass to gypsiferous clays likewise full of bipyramidal quartz.

In the upper part of this formation, and near the windmill, occasionally a solitary crystal of sulphur is seen imbedded in one of the numerous geodes found within the rock.

When this rock is broken the workmen who quarry them affirm that a strong smell of sulphuretted hydrogen is occassionally perceived.

In section N.º 13 another very similar phenomenon will be observed.

On leaving the River Zurraque towards the Salineta de Guerra, the Pliocene formation will be seen greatly disturbed and dipping about 38 deprees to the N. W., and before reaching the fold marked A in the section, the totality of the Tertiary series is passed.

The white Nummulitic marls are coloured by red oxide of iron, and at about 50 meters from the gypsums and dolomites in the anticlinal axis, only traces of magnesia exist in the rock; whilst from this point this substance gradually augments, and when at about two meters from the gypsiferous clays, the rock is much more dense and compact; and from 15 to 20 per cent of that substance is found. It nevertheless always possesses an aspect similar to the original marls. Shortly this similarity disappears; the rock on one side becomes cellular, whilst on the other its coherance is lost and passes to variegated clays till it definitively subsides to the normal gypsiferous formation.

This phenomenon is repeated in the series of folds of the strata in this locality. The gradual passage which is constantly observed between the Tertiary deposits and the gypsiferous strata is extremely remarkable.

N.⁰ 14 is also a very interesting section, and it would be difficult to explain it if we accepted that the whole of these deposits formed part of a simultaneous sedimentary deposit.

From Port Royal to the lime quarries or Caleras, a distance of about two kilometers, the strata are doubly folded, one of the crests passing by the above mentioned lime quarries and the other by the hill known under the name of Cerro de Ceuta.

The synclinal axis between the Cerro de Ceuta and the quarries is formed by the Pliocene sands: on the side of the Ceuta hill these sands pass to the Miocene clays, which pass directly to the gypsiferous formation, whilst the white Nummulitic marls appear on the side of the quarries.

Before the Tertiary clays pass to the gypsums of the Ceuta hill (all the Eocene deposits apparently wanting in such a short distance) the clays alternate with layers of Carbonate of lime; at times crystallized, when they are accompanied by Sulphate of Strontia.

The gypsums in this place tend to prove a most remarkable fact. Imbedded in the variegated clays there are found numerous blocks and layers of a marly white limestone exactly similar to the white Nummulitic marls which outcrop a short distance from them.

These blocks are intimately united to the clays and gypsums, and they pass to them through insensible gradations. Large needles of cristalized gypsum penetrate them towards their centre, and it is difficult not to see in them the Nummulitic marls in which the metamorphic action has not been sufficient to completely obliterate their original characters.

In the same Ceuta Hill and about three hundred meters from the place from where the above mentioned phenomenon occurs, there exist layers and patches of sandstones, sometimes alternating and at other times intimately mixed with clays and marmorean limestones. In some places of the same strata the sandstone is of a deep red color and a piece of the rock seen isolated might be mistaken .for an old red sandstone rock; whilst in other places it is a yellow friable sandstone with impressions of plants and casts of small shells in an inferior state of preservation; but amongst which however Mr. Etheridge has been able to recognize a Panopea, a Cardium and an Unicardium, which he considers decidedly Cretaceous.

All these clays and sandstones are full of crystallized aragonite, sometimes in beautiful radiated concretions, filling the casts of the shells; and others in rather stout hexagonal prisms of more than two centimeters in length.

A spot between Paterna and Medina is also worthy of observation, for the gypsums alternate with sandstones which have exactly the appearance of the sandstones which constitute the hills of Medina, and which as it has been shewn belong to the upper Eocene or to the Miocene formation.

When describing the Miocene calcareous conglomerate of Espera, I have already referred to their semi crystallized state, whilst at a short distance to the W. S. W. near the rivulet named Arroyo del Salitre, a patch of gypsiferous clays outcrop in the midst of the Miocene clays, shewing the correspondence which exists between the two phenomena.

Between Puerto Real and Paterna, especially between the Puerto de Buena Vista and the Laguna del Taraje, there are large tracts of ground in which it is extremely difficult to decide whether they belong to the Tertiary series or whether they are to be considered as appertaining to the gypsiferous formation.

These deposits are so intimately connected with the Tertiary series that it is almost impossible to separate both formations, and this same remarkable fact is repeated in all the sedimentary deposits of this Province through which the ophites have outcropped.

In the Berrueco Hill for instance an extraordinary example occurs. Section N.º 16, shows the strange position of the different strata, supposing this gypsiferous formation to be a sedimentary deposit, for in such a short distance the gypsiferous marls are in contact with the Nummulitic marls, with the Neocomian marls and with the inferior white marbles; and the whole of these deposits pass through the identical insensible gradations to the gypsums and dolomites.

In the Sierra del Valle and neighbouring hills, the passages from the Cretaceous rocks to the gypsiferous deposits are also worthy of note.

In the locality called La Cierva there exists a very anomalous section, as is shewn in section N.º9.

This hill is formed on its Northern slopes towards the valley of the Garganta de los Toreros by the Cretaceous deposits, whilst its summit is crowned by nearly vertical slabs of Nummulitic limestone.

On descending by the southern slopes of the hill towards the Garganta de Pajarete, the Nummulitic formation passes to the gypsum deposits; and the Neocomian formation is altogether wanting, till it is seen in the Dehesa La Dorada to the east of Jigonza reposing on the gypsums and variegated clays.

In Prado de Rey and El Bosque the same phenomenon is repeated; here however it is not limited to the Neocomian deposits, for the red Jurassic marbles pass to the gypsiferous deposits; whilst in Benamahoma and Ubrique the ophites are seen to protrude under the Liassic formation with the invariably dependant gypsums and dolomites.

From what precedes it will be seen that the gypsiferous deposits outcrop in the midst of all the geological series of this Province, and always the same gradual passage from one deposit to the other is observed.

In the face of these facts are we justified in considering the totality of these deposits as Triassic?

Is it not more probable that this formation is the result of a mineralizing action which has taken place during the folding of the strata and which accompanied the eruption of the Ophites?

A very similar phenomenon to this exists in the outcropings of ophites which are seen on both sides of the Pyrenees and which warrant the latter opinion.

The ophites of the Pyrenees appear with the same constant association of gypsums and variegated marls; they likewise protrude amidst the most varied formations; and the majority of Geologists who have studied them are unanimous in considering these gypsiferous marls as in inmediate dependance to the ophites.

Besides this, we ought to bear in mind that M. Bouvy who has studied the Island of Mallorca, has found reasons to consider that its actual relief is due to the eruption of porphyrs, on the contact of which the limestones have been altered to gypsums and cipolins, and as this Island is in the E. N. E. extreme of the phenomenon I am describing, it is highly probable that what he has there observed is part of this same phenomenon.

If we admit that this formation is the result of a metamorphic action, the problem which naturally presents itself for solution is the difficult one of ascertaining how natural forces have acted in producing this phenomenon.

I have not the slightest pretensions to present a theory for explaining the subject, but perhaps it will help to more thoroughly understanding it, if I emit the impressions which its study has produced in my mind.

Considering the series of foldings which this part of the continent has experienced and which have so greatly reduced the space originally occupied by the different strata, and the enormous pressures which they must have experienced; and considering that the ophites and gypsums occupy the anticlinal axis of the folds, it is natural to infer that these ophites broke through the crests of these folds as these were the sites of lesser resistance in the strata.

Probably during the very long period in which the folding of the strata took place (a circumstance which is proved by the fragments of the Pliocene deposits appearing in the upper part of the some formation), part of the strata on both sides of the anticlinal fractures experienced the action of thermal waters, or of this same substance as steam, and more or less saturated with different mineralizing substances; which gradually impregnated them and gradually transformed them to what they are at present.

This action I fancy would have been similar to that which would have taken place in a volcanic focus in which, either through the structure of the ground or through any other cause, no communication could have been established with the atmosphere. It would then probably occur that the gases through not losing the enormous tension which they possessed at a certain depth below the surface would produce reactions very similar to those which are observed in this region. In this case the gases or mineral waters would gradually permeate the strata, and originate different reactions dependant on their different composition and structure. Sometimes they would dissolve the strata, whilst at other times they would infiltrate in them new substances, which before had no existance, and this probably slow action would continue through periods of perhaps enormous length and give rise to numerous epigenesis; so varied, that those known in our laboratories are perhaps only a small 'fraction of those which may take place in the great laboratory of Nature.

The facts however already known are sufficient to establish the possibility at least of these epigenesis.

The well known and beautiful experiments of M. Daubree with superheated water in close vessels, as well as the possibility of producing variegated clays when vapours of water and hidrochloric acid are successively passed through ferruginous clays: the experiments of M. Senarmont on the production of anhydrous oxide of iron in solutions of common salt at temperatures between 160 to 180 cent: those of MM. Sainte Claire Deville Bischoff and others, as also the highly interesting ones of M. II. Sterry Hunt on the decomposition of Sulphate of Magnesia by Bicarbonate of lime, and those of M. Haidinger on the action of Sulphate of Magnesia at high temperature on the limestones, which transforms them into gypsums and dolomites, throw great light on the phenomena which have apparently taken place in this Province.

DESCRIPTION OF THE GENERAL SECTIONS
AND OF THE DISTURBANCES WHICH HAVE TAKEN PLACE IN THE
PROVINCE OF CADIZ.

When for the first time the state of violent disturbance in which the whole of the strata of this Province is observed, it appears scarcely possible to discover the law to which they obey.

For instance the Pliocene deposits present the following anomalies; in Cadiz they dip 20 degrees to the E. S. E.

whilst between Port Royal and Medina they dip 38 degrees to the N. W. and in Port St. Marys and Port Royal they frequently dip to the S. W. or N. E.

This apparent confusion is still more striking in the strata inferior to the Pliocene deposits, for as it will be easily perceived on studying the structure of the country, these deposits generally occupy the synclinal axis of the folds; and therefore they hardly ever appear in the vicinity of the ophites, where the greatest disturbances have taken place.

I more especially refer to the Tertiary series, for though the same phenomenon is observed in the Secondary deposits, as they have apparently been disturbed prior to the Tertiary epoch they ought, to be studied separately.

The dip and strike of the strata of this Province vary in the extreme: sometimes they dip to the N. or N. W. or W., with an inclination which varies from the vertical to nearly horizontal; and at other times their dip changes from S. to E. with the same difference in the amount of the dip; whilst in the strata that remained horizontal between the anticlinal axis of the folds, their dip is frequently to the S. W. or N. E.

To better understand however the structure of this region I will refer the reader to sections N.º 16, 17, 18 and 19.

These sections are parallel to each other, and cut the Province from N. W. to S. E. in a plane almost perpendicular to the stratification.

The first of these sections follows the direction of the coast from the Island of Leon to the banks of the River Barbate near its mouth to the South of Cape Trafalgar.

The second cuts the Province from the River Zurraque to the west of the Vega de Guerra to the Janda Lake, passing by the Berrueco, and the third shows the structure of the country comprized between the Pico del Algibe and the vicinity of Arcos; whilst the fourth shows the longitudinal section of the mountains to the N. E. of the Province.

In sections Nos. 16 and 17 the distances are $\frac{1}{50.000}$ of the natural ones and the altitudes $\frac{1}{12.500}$; whilst in Nos. 18 and 19 both distances and altitudes are $\frac{1}{50.000}$.

DESCRIPTION OF SECTION N.º 16.

This section commences, as already stated, in the vicinity of the town of San Fernando in the Island of Leon, where a patch of the Pliocene formation is found protruding from amongst the modern clays of Cadiz Bay, which in the direction of this section extend to the town of Chiclana.

In the Pinewood close to this town the Pliocene deposits reappear covered by the diluvium. From this place to the base of the Santa Ana hill the whole of the Tertiary deposits dipping to the N. W. may by observed.

At a short distance from the base of this hill, specially on the road which leads from Chiclana to the Fuente Amarga sulphurous springs, the white Nummulitic marls are seen to pass to an outcrop of gypsiferous marls, on both sides of which the dip of the strata is reversed.

From this place to the Pinar del Hierro the strata appear with two very rapid folds, in the first of which very thick beds of gypsum are seen, whilst in the one nearest to the Pinewood the Nummulitic limestones outcrop, with an extraordinary abundance of Nummulites.

In the Pinewood the Pliocene deposits are again found likewise covered by the diluvium.

From this place to the Puerto de la Lobita the country forms an extensive tract of almost level ground, which near the Puerto reaches nearly 90 meters above the sea. When the Puerto is passed, the ground rapidly descends to the valley of the Salado de Conil, which river runs only at about 15 meters above the sea.

At the bottom of the valley there exists a highly decomposed outcrop of ophite accompanied by large deposits of gypsums and dolomites, on both sides of which the dip of the strata is reversed.

From this outcrop of ophite to the upper part of the Altos de Patria the whole of the Tertiary formation is seen.

One of the sites where the gradual transition in the dip of the strata already referred to can be observed is in the cuttings on the highway to Veger and in the numerous places where the strata protrude.

The Altos de Patria form an extensive tableland 160 meters above the sea and covered by the diluvial deposits.

Between these heights and Veger another anticlinal axis is passed; the Miocene strata on descending the Altos de Patria towards Veger are seen to dip to the N. W., whilst the same strata disappear under the Pliocene deposits, which constitute the hills on the left bank of the Barbate, with a S. E. dip.

DESCRIPTION OF SECTION N.º 17.

On leaving the Pinewoods, half way between Port Royal and the Berrueco hill, and on the banks of the river Zurraque the Pliocene deposits are seen with a dip of 38 degrees to the N. W.

From this place to the Salineta de Guerra the dip of the strata appears to be constantly to the N. W. and from hence to the watershed of the rivers Iro and Zurraque, the strata is found, as already stated when describing Section N.º 13, in four consecutive folds with powerful gypsum deposits in the anticlinal axis.

In the upper part of the watershed the Nummulitic formation is seen, but on descending to the valley of the Iro the gypsiferous strata reappear and are not lost till the cretaceous rocks of the already described Berrueco are reached. In the interval two outcrops of ophite are found.

On the southern base of this rock the gypsiferous clays again make their appearance, though for a short distance, for in the neighbouring Cerro de la Espartosa the Nummulitic strata are again met with, crowning the summit of the hill.

On descending its southern slopes a considerable outcrop of ophite is seen, and it is worthy of note how distinctly the strata have their dip reversed on both sides of this ophite.

From this place to the Pico del Aguila two more outcrops of ophite are met with, and between them a considerable extent of the inferior Nummulitic deposits are passed.

The Pico del Aguila is constituted at its base by the inferior Nummulitic deposits, while its summit is crowned by the upper sandstones.

On descending the southern slopes of this hill, the Nummulitic limestones are again found, and pass to the gypsiferous clays which accompany another outcrop of ophite. In connection with this ophite a very extraordinary circumstance is observed.

Whilst in the slopes of the Pico del Aguila the inferior limestones are seen between the sandstones and the gypsums, on the other side of the fold the gypsums appear in contact with the upper sandstones.

Instead of continuing the section in a straight line from the south of the Pico del Aguila it is transported somewhat to the E. N. E.; and following the same anticlinal axis, the section is continued from the place called Dehesa Arenales to the Mountains on the left bank of the Barbate.

At about one and a half kilometers before reaching the Molino de Badalejo, the sandstone strata are seen to dip to the N. W., below which the inferior Nummulitic limestones reappear, but they shortly after change their dip to the S. E.; and again disappear under the upper sandstones at about half a kilometer before reaching the Mesa de Casas Viejas. Close to the highest part of the Mesa the sandstones pass to a calcareous conglomerate, identical to the one found in the Altos de Patria.

The Mesa forms an extensive tableland at about 90 or 100 meters above the sea. It measures nearly four kilometers from North to South and is completely covered by the diluvial deposits, under which it is highly probable the Pliocene deposits will be found.

Before reaching Casas Viejas the calcareous conglomerate is again seen dipping to the N. W.; and at the base of the Mesa and near the low grounds of the Janda Lake the sandstones reappear.

These sandstones are lost under the modern deposits of this lake, though only for a short distance; for in the neighbouring Sierra de los Tahones they are again seen with a very decided dip to the S. E.

DESCRIPTION OF SECTION N.º 18.

In the sulphur deposits of Arcos, at about 5 kilometers to the west of this town, the Tertiary strata are seen highly impregnated with this substance, and reposing on the gypsiferous clays seen at a short distance from the road to Arcos in the bed of the Salado de Espera. From this place to Arcos, as already mentioned, the whole Tertiary series is seen.

The town of Arcos is built on the Pliocene deposits; which on the right bank of the Guadalete form a perpendicular wall of more than 100 meters in vertical height.

These deposits repose on the calcareous conglomerate already described.

From this place to the Sierra Rabita, this conglomerate alternates with the Pliocene sands; but on reaching the valley of the Arroyo Mazagan, the white Nummulitic marls make their appearance and pass to the gypsums and dolomites at the bottom of the valley. These gypsums form an anticlinal axis, for whilst the strata of the Sierra Rabita dip to the N. W. those of the Sierra de Aznar on the other side of the valley dip to the S. E.

From the base of this Sierra to about three kilometers before reaching Algar the Tertiary deposits are met with; but from this place to the banks of the River Majaccite one of the most violent disturbed regions is passed. Three consecutive outcrops of ophite are met with, and the foldings of the strata between these rocks are extremely pronounced.

At a short distance from the ruined Castle of Tempul, built on the last of these outcrops of ophites, the gypsiferous deposits disappear under the Secondary limestones of the Sierra de las Cabras.

This Sierra is constituted by a series of most rapid folds and its isolated form, as already stated, is extremely remarkable.

In the southern extremity of this Sierra, in the place called Puerto de las Palomas, a considerable outcrop of ophite is seen in the midst of the secondary deposits, and accompanied with the corresponding gypsiferous clays.

At the base of the Picacho the Secondary strata disappear under the Nummulitic limestones, which at a short distance also disappear under the potent formation of sandstones of this part of the Sierra.

From the base of the Picacho to the Pico del Algibe the Sierra is constituted by a synclinal axis between this outcrop of ophite and the anticlinal axis, which at the base of the Pico in the Peñas de Armes, forces the Cretaceous rocks again to protrude from under the Nummulitic beds which at a short distance dip to the S. E. and disappear again under the sandstones. These folds follow each other in rapid succession in the direction of the Straits of Gibraltar.

DESCRIPTION OF SECTION N.º 19.

This section shows the structure of one of the most important groups of the Ronda Mountains. It extends from the vicinity of Prado de Rey to the Sierra de Libar.

At the small chapel of Nuestra Señora de las Montañas to the N. W. of Prado de Rey, the Jurassic red marbles are seen covered by the series of deposits with Terebratula Janitor which constitute the hills of the Sierra de la Espuela, on the summits of which the Nummulitic limestones are seen at nearly 600 meters above the sea. In front of these hills the Sierra del Pinar towers as the culminating point of the Province; and the depression between them is called the Puerto del Algamazon, at the bottom of which a series of ophites and gypsiferous deposits are seen.

The Sierra del Pinar raises abruptly from the Puerto del Algamazon, and between this Puerto and that of El Pinar it constitutes a mass of Secondary limestone cleft in its centre by a fault, which on the side nearest to the Sierra Blanquilla uplifts the Liassic strata to a higher level than the red Jurassic marbles attain, and which appear to dip under the Liassic deposits.

It is highly probable that the abrupt elevation of the Sierra from the Puerto del Algamazon, may be due to another break in the strata which may have placed them in the anomalous position they now present.

The Puerto del Pinar is formed by the anticlinal axis of a fold which has raised the contact of the Liassic limestones with the shales to more than 1100 meters above the sea.

In this part of the Sierra the strata have not only been bent and folded; but they have been also bodily upheaved. At the bottom of the steep ravine which leads to the upper part of the Puerto, and quite close to the village of Benamahoma, the contact between these two deposits near the outcrop of ophite is hardly 500 meters above the sea, whilst from this place on ascending the stream to the upper part of the Puerto which follows the anticlinal axis of the fold, the contact between the Liassic limestones and the shales is gradually seen to rise; and at the upper part of the Puerto they are more than 1100 meters above the sea.

Between this place and the Puerto del Boyal the structure of the Sierra is very extraordinary. The strata is here seen in an extremely inclined fold which raises the Liassic shales to more than 1300 meters above the sea in the vicinity of the Peñon de San Cristobal; whilst on the side of the Puerto del Boyal a great rent, similar to the one observed between the Puerto del Algamazon and the Puerto del Pinar, seems to have taken place; which accounts for the extraordinary state in which the strata are found here.

In this opening of the Sierra a patch of the Nummulitic deposits is seen occupying this highly compressed synclinal axis, but it is so much altered and laminated, that it is difficult to recognize it. The strata of this formation are mostly vertical, and sometimes they are seen to dip apparently under the Jurassic limestones. The sandstones which constitute it are so much changed that they are frequently transformed to extremely compact green jaspers; and variegated clays and gypsums are seen to penetrate both the Nummulitic and Jurassic formations. The whole of the strata in this part of the Sierra frequently appear as if they had been ground to dust.

The summits of the Sierra from the Puerto del Boyal to the Sierra de Libar are formed by the upper Jurassic deposits.

These mountains constitute a succession of folds, some of which cause the Liassic limestones and shales to protrude to a considerable height, as it can be seen for instance near Ubrique.

The last of these folds constitutes the curious pass of the Manga de Villaluenga, which separates the Sierra del Endrinal from the Sierra de Libar already in the vicinity of Ronda.

The upper Jurassic marbles having been broken by this last folding of the strata; the soft red shales form the nearly level depression of this dreary defile.

It is thus seen that by whichever place we cut this Province from N. W. to S. E. an identical structure is 'observed. It is an established fact that its strata have been violently folded in a direction almost at right angles to the one followed.

This phenomenon appears to have taken place in an extremely modern epoch, and this is sufficiently proved by the strictly corresponding upheaval of the Pliocene.

As it has been shewn by the above mentioned sections, the whole of the geological series of this Province have been profoundly disturbed, and to such an extent, as to completely mask the unconformity of stratification of the Tertiary and Secondary strata, which undoubtedly exists; as everywhere proofs are seen of profound disturbances in the Secondary strata prior to the Tertiary epoch.

In the Ronda Mountains it is frequent to observe the Tertiary deposits leaning against the Secondary limestones, which evidently formed high cliffs when those deposits were being formed. This is amply demonstrated by the large blocks of Secondary limestones imbedded in the base of those ancient cliffs.

If these sections are attentively examined, it will be found that the different anticlinal and synclinal axis of the different folds will correspond with each other if they be prolonged in the direction E. 28 N.

If for instance, the hardly disturbed strata' to the south of the Pinar del Hierro are prolonged to the E. 28 N. it will be seen that in this band, not only are the synclinal axis which constitute the Jarales of Medina Hills comprized; but likewise that portion of the Sierra del Algibe which lies between the Picacho and the Pico del Algibe.

If the Pliocene beds of the Pinar del Hierro are also prolonged with the same direction, this band will not only comprise the Nummulitic hills to the South of the Berrueco and the Hills of Medina; but likewise the Southern extremity of the Sierra de las Cabras.

If instead of this, the series of rapid folds which the strata present between Chiclana and the Pinar del Hierro are prolonged, they will not only pass by the disturbed strata of the Berrueco;

but they will also correspond to the series of violent folds of the Sierra de las Cabras and the Sierra del Endrinal.

This parallelism will be still more s'riking if we study the direction which the ophites follow.

At the base of the Berroquejo, which is a small Cretaceous hill to the west of Paterna, an outcrop of ophite exists. If through this place a line parallel to the direction A B in the chart is drawn it will unite the following points.

The anticlinal axis of the Puerto del Pinar, the ophite in Benamahoma; the fold of the Sierra de Albarracin; the ophites and gypsums of El Bosque; the great outcrop of ophite to the North of the Pasada de la Plata; the gypsums and disturbed strata of the Puerto de la Cruz; and the ophite to the south of the Laguna del Taraje.

If through the Castle of Tempul another parallel line is drawn, it will likewise follow a constantly dislocated ground the principal points of which are the following.

The vertical strata seen on leaving Grazalema on the way to Ronda; the protuberance of the Sierra del Valle; and the series of dislocated and gypsiferous clays which when following this direction are passed between this Sierra and the Salineta de Guerra.

I have observed with more or less precision fourteen of these anticlinal axis between Cadiz Bay and Cape Trafalgar; and this number is sufficient to prove the magnitude of the phenomenon I am describing.

·The most remarkable fact is that the lowest valleys of the Province are invariably found on following these anticlinal axis; but as this subject is closely related to another fact of capital importance I will describe it before proceeding any further.

When the strata which were scarcely disturbed in the synclinal axis of the folds, as well as the deposits more recent than the Pliocene are observed, they are frequently seen to dip sometimes to the S. W. and others to the N. E. and this dip sometimes reaches 20 or 25 degrees.

It is evident that the strata which have been upheaved obeying the folding motion ought generally to have their maximum of dip to the S. S. E. or N. N. W.; but instead of this it oscillates round this direction; sometimes dipping to the S., S. E., E. S. E., or E. and others to the N., N. W., W. N. W. and W. and it is worthy of remark that the greater the primitive deviation from the horizontal, the lesser is the deviation.

This state of the strata proves that after the folding action had ceased, this country again experienced another disturbing motion exactly at right angles to the previous one; the natural result of which has been to give to the totality of the strata of this Province the resultant dip of these two disturbances.

This supposition acquires the evidence of a fact when the structure of this region, especially of its southern extremity, is observed.

When describing the form of the coast of this Province I mentioned the series of parallel lines which give it shape.

In the orographical description I have likewise called attention to the series of transverse valleys which cross the entire Province from N. N. W. to S. S. E.

If the isometrical chart which accompanies this paper is attentively observed, it will be seen that this series of valleys are not only parallel to the direction of the coast, but perpendicular to the anticlinal axis of the folds.

The epoch in which these valleys have been formed is extremely recent.

No better proof is required of this fact than the position the diluvial deposits occupy on the summits of the hills, whilst in the lower parts of the valleys I have never seen any traces of them.

Crossing the Province on its western extremity, the first valley we meet is the deep and shallow depression through which the River Barbate flows in the latter part of its course.

This valley runs parallel to the general direction of the coast from S. S. E. to N. N. W. between the heights of Veger and the Sierra de Retin, and the summits of all these heights are formed by a nearly level tract of ground which in the Sierra de Retin rises to nearly 400 meters above the sea.

This valley not only comprises the bed of the Barbate, but it extends to the N. N. W. through the depression between the Altos de Patria and the Mesa de Veger to the low grounds near the Bay of Cadiz.

The second of these transversal valleys which appears is the extensive depression which constitutes the Janda Lake in winter.

This valley is evidently the assemblage of a series of minor valleys, which in the extreme south of the Province are observed; and which, blended together in this place, form this depression.

In the intervening space between the mouth of the Barbate and the Punta Tarifa five remarkable depressions are seen.

The first of these is the considerable one which intervenes between the Sierra de Retin and the protuberances of the Sierra de la Plata and Silla del Papa.

Between the group of wild rocks which constitute the Silla del Papa and the Sierra de San Mateo another abrupt depression is met with; and from this last Sierra to the Sierra de la Luna three more succesive depressions occur.

It is extremely interesting to observe the structure of this part of the country. It is constituted by a series of abrupt and savage mountains from 600 to 800 meters in height, separated by a series of parallel valleys in some places almost at the sea level, and which are perpendicular to the direction of the folds which constitute these mountains.

Their crests are formed of the upper Tertiary sandstones, whilst in the lower part of the valleys the inferior Nummulitic deposits are found.

This extraordinary structure is no where seen to a greater advantage than in the Puerto de Facinas between the Sierras de Enmedio and San Mateo, where the inferior Nummulitic strata are seen to cross the valley from one mountain to the other uniting the respective folds.

After crossing the group of high Sierras to the east of the Janda lake, another similar valley is met with, which though equally deep in some places, does not form the extensive tract of level ground of the Janda depression in its lower part.

This depression is extremely well defined and by a series of parallel valleys, it can be traced for more than 80 kilometers from the banks of the Guadalete to the Bay of Gibraltar.

The next great depression met with is the valley through

which the River Guadarranque runs. In the series of fractures which constitute this valley; the valleys are narrower and a certain want of continuity is observed.

The valleys here though depressed are not so broad as those of the Janda Lake. The Protuberance of the Algibe shows a more moderate action; though yet sufficient to produce the elongated and anomalous mass of the Sierra de las Cabras.

The last of these great transversal valleys which may be traced in this Province is the gap through which the Rivers Guadiaro and Hoz garganta flow in the latter part of their course.

This break though not so strikingly marked as those already described is of extreme importance; as it shews that we are receding from the place where this extraordinary disturbance was initiated.

I therefore consider it is an established fact that this country has been violently folded in a series of parallel folds in a posterior epoch to the Pliocene deposits; and that after the diluvium was deposited and previous to the crests of the folds having been degraded to their actual level, another extremely profound disturbance was experienced.

This disturbance I imagine similar to the distortion which an iron bar would experience if, when firmly held by one of its extremities, it supported on the other a weight superior to its force of flexion. It would then happen that the small fissures generated on its surface perpendicular to its length would well represent the fissured state of the strata of this country at that period.

These fissures and gaps once formed would naturally be, through atmospheric agencies, scooped down to their present level.

If all these facts are united to those put forward when describing the diluvial deposit of the Province, there will be more than presumptive grounds for supposing that the focus from whence this extraordinary disturbance has arisen is to be found at some distance in the Atlantic.

We cannot otherwise explain those transverse valleys, which become more and more decided the nearer we approach the western coasts. Those diluvial deposits close to the seaside elevated nearly two hundred meters above its level, nor the inmense quantities of rolled pebbles of quarzite, for the origin of which we cannot now a days satisfactorily account.

The series of disturbances I have described have had a most important influence in the actual orographical structure of this Province.

They explain the disjointed and anomalous structure of the Ronda Mountains; for it is evident that two disturbances which cut each other at nearly right angles, are extremely appropriate to produce a system of disconnected mountains which is their distinguishing feature.

The mountains from the N. E. of the Province to the Punta Tarifa, which approximately follow the diagonal of the parallelogram constructed with these two directions, do not exclusively obey to the folding and fracture movement.

As a consequence of the metamorphic action which accompanied the first disturbance, the erosions have tended to follow the crest of the primitive folds.

This cause united to the repeated folding of the strata would suffice to produce a sufficiently complicated orographical structure without the new disturbance which has cut all connection between the various chains of mountains, producing all this jumble of high summits and deep defiles alternating with plains and table lands, which constitute this part of the Betic chain.

I do not however pretend to say that the relief of this complicated Serrania is the result only of these two last disturbances.

As I have more than once stated, the Secondary deposits had, previous to the Tertiary epoch, been sufficiently upheaved to form at least a protuberance of sufficient dimensions to greatly influence the currents and sediments of those seas.

When describing the Betic Chain, I have also pointed out the difference of direction between the central and the litoral chains which blend in the Ronda Mountains, as well, as referred to the difference of composition of their strata.

I believe, therefore, that besides the important part which the disturbances I have described have had on the present relief of the Ronda Mountains, those which previously at least

partially upheaved the Penibetic Chain, have also greatly influenced their actual structure.

The folding of the strata appears to have extended over considerable ground, and though I have not sufficiently studied the
whole of Andalusia so as to possess the necessary amount of facts,
certain coincidences are worthy of being taken into account.

If a line is drawn from the last outcrop of gypsums seen in
the road between Cadiz and Seville at Lebrija and the Cabezas
de San Juan to the first outcrop of these same rocks, seen on the
road from Cordoba to Malaga between Aguilar and Montilla, it
will be found that this line is, strangely enough, parallel to the direction E. 28 N. which as repeatedly stated is the direction the
folds of the Province follow.

On observing M. M. Verneuil and Collombs Geological Chart
of the Peninsula it is also extremely remarkable to find the Secondary and Nummulitic bands of Andalusia likewise parallel to
this direction.

If we draw another line parallel to this band through the last
outcrops of ophites near Conil, this line will cut the Mountains of
the Province of Malaga in the vicinity of the Gaitanes pass, to
the north of which the gypsiferous deposits begin to make their
appearance, whilst to the south numerous faults and considerable
outcrops of serpentine are visible.

These folds in the extreme south of the Province have generally a very small radius, and are frequently in V form; but as they
approach the valley of the Guadalquivir they gradually enlargen
and measure from three to four kilometers from crest to crest.

On reaching this river these folds gradually dissappear, and in
the first offshoots of the Sierra Morena the Tertiary strata are
scarcely disturbed.

From the straits of Gibraltar to the valley of the Guadalquivir therefore a gradual diminution of the intensity of this phenomenon is observed.

When we consider the magnitude of the disturbance to which
the Alps owe the most important part of their relief, and the inmense portion of the earths surface which appears to have been
affected by this modern fracture: when we see the extent of strata

recently disturbed through this enormous upheaval which from the Himalaya to the Alps has everywhere left its traces; and when we find the phenomenon observed in this Province exactly in its prolongation, and terminating likewise after the most recent Tertiary stra'a were deposited; I do not think it unreasonable to suppose that the folds seen in this locality are an accidental part of that immense series of fractures.

When these highly compressed strata are seen interposed between the Atlas Mountains on the South and the elevated table lands of Spain on the North, I cannot refrain from considering that a certain correspondence between both facts exists.

On regarding the series of folds of the strata gradually disappear in the valley of the Guadalquivir, whilst on its right bank the Sierra Morena rises with its ladder like structure; which can only be explained by admitting a series of faults, perhaps coincident with the partial upheaval of the Spanish plateau; and when finally the direction which this mountain chain follows is observed, which is from E. N. E. to W. S. W. this correspondence is yet more fully established, and the reason of the gradual diminishing of the folding of the strata may be explained by the partial upheaval of the Spanish table lands, which relieved these highly compressed strata of the pressure they at that time experienced.

Unhappily however nothing but more or less well grounded hypothesis are possible, considering the scanty data we possess for solving this problem.

Notwithstanding this, I consider it is evident that the folding of the strata of this Province is not an isolated phenomenon, but on the contrary connected with one of those great disturbances of our globe, which though effected in longer or shorter periods, have everlastingly impressed its action on the surface of our planet.

If we are to judge by the fractures at right angles to the folds, it is highly probable that these disturbances were prolonged to the epoch when our ancestors were in a sufficiently advanced state of intellectual development to allow its last effects to remain permanently engraved on their minds.

It is sufficiently demonstrated that these fractures and lever motion took place in an extremely modern epoch, but there is a fact which gives still greater weight to this inference.

Mixed with the innumerable rolled pebbles of quarzite, which characterize the diluvial deposits, I have found in the Chiclana Pinewood a polished greenstone implement; a small wedge or hatchet almost triangular in shape.

The felspar of this stone is strangely enough completely decomposed; probably owing to the mineralizing action of the diluvial waters, the red deposits of which indicate that they were in a different state to those which now commonly flow on the earths surface.

It appears therefore that the race which employed the stone implements, of which the one I have gathered is a specimen, witnessed the phenomena which produced and accompanied the extraordinary disturbance which this part of the world experienced after the diluvial deposits.

As I have already stated it is highly probable that the records of the legendary Atlantida were the reminiscences of this violent commotion, which would naturally persistently subsist for a lengthened time even in the weak minds of those who were perhaps our prehistoric ancestors; and whose country at present, or a portion of it at least, may be beneath the waters of the Atlantic Ocean.